TO THE LIMIT
MOUNTAIN BIKING

Paul Mason

PowerKiDS
press.
New York

Published in 2012 by the Rosen Publishing Group Inc.
29 East 21st Street, New York, NY 10010

First Edition

Produced for Wayland by Roger Coote Publishing,
Gissing's Farm, Fressingfield, Eye, Suffolk IP21 5SH
Project Management: Mason Editorial Services
Designer: Tim Mayer

Photographs: All photos supplied by John Kitchiner/**mbr** magazine except page 9 br Paul Mason; page 11 Gary Fisher © 2008 Trek Bicycle Corporation; page 27 Giuseppe Cacace/Stringer/Getty Images.

Library of Congress Cataloging-in-Publication Data

Mason, Paul, 1967–
  Mountain biking / by Paul Mason. — 1st ed.
     p. cm. — (To the limit)
  Includes index.
  ISBN 978-1-4488-7028-8 (library binding) — ISBN 978-1-4488-7064-6 (pbk.) — ISBN 978-1-4488-7065-3 (6-pack)
  1. Mountain biking—Juvenile literature. I. Title.
  GV1056.M37 2012
  796.63—dc23

                              2011028891

Manufactured in Malaysia

CPSIA Compliance Information: Batch #WW2102PK: For Further Information contact Rosen Publishing, New York, New York at 1-800-237-9932

CONTENTS

WARNING!

Mountain biking is a dangerous sport. This book is full of advice, but reading it won't keep you safe on the mountain. Take responsibility for your own safety. You should always wear a helmet when doing any kind of mountain biking. Always ride safely and wear your helmet!

WHAT IS MOUNTAIN BIKING?

Mountain biking's thrills are summed up by the excitement of racing at top speed down a trail that's wide enough for only one rider, trying to catch up to a disappearing friend (or trying to stay ahead of a friend who's desperately trying to catch you).

This kind of single-track riding, as it's called, is sought out by mountain bikers all around the world. But there are plenty of other thrills in mountain biking, of course. There are jumps, downhill rides, cross country, dual slalom races, and 24-hour relay races. In fact, too many different kinds of mountain-bike activity to list here.

Bikers enjoying a day far from the city.

The Secret Language of Mountain Biking

Drop-off   A vertical or near-vertical descent.

Dual slalom When two riders race side-by-side down a preset course.

Fire road   A wide track through a forest, originally built as access for large trucks or fire engines.

Freeride   Riding anywhere you want to, along a route that's a fun mixture of single track, jumps, climbs, and mor[e]

Full-sus   Short for full suspension: a bike that has suspension for the front and rear wheels.

Hardtail   A bike with suspension forks on the front but a rigid rear.

Travel   The amount of movement in a suspension system: a bike whose forks move 3 inches (80 mm) is said to have 3 inches (80 mm) travel.

Trials   When riders perform tricks on their bikes while moving around a prearranged set of obstacles.

Mountain biking is about freedom. It's about escape and adventure… When you get to the end of the trail and look back, you say to yourself, "Whoa! I just did that." It's a real adrenaline rush.

- *Gary Klein, mountain-bike pioneer, explains why he got into the sport in the first place.*

5

BACK WHEN IT ALL BEGAN

Mountain biking started in California. A group of friends got together a bunch of old beach cruisers and drove up to the top of their local mountain with the bikes in a pickup truck. Then they raced each other back down again. "This is fun: let's do it again!" they thought, and mountain biking had been born. The sport spread and spread, until 20 years or so after that first run there were more mountain bikes being sold than any other kind.

"**A** thoroughly useful maintenance manual that also happens to be great fun to read."
— Jim Langley, *Bicycling* magazine

ZINN and the ART of MOUNTAIN BIKE MAINTENANCE

By Lennard Zinn
Senior Technical Writer of VeloNews

The Godfathers of Mountain Biking

The Californian youngsters who first started mountain biking realized the bikes they had been using weren't really that good. Some of them started building their own bikes.

Today, these are some of the biggest names in the mountain-biking industry: Gary Fisher, Keith Bontrager, Tom Ritchey, and Gary Klein have all given their names to successful companies.

Jargon Buster

Coaster brakes Brakes that are part of the back wheel: you pedal backwards to slow down.

Beach cruiser A relaxed style of bike with no gears, coaster brakes, and big, fat tires.

The bikes have changed since the early days of mountain biking, but the thrill is the same.

Taiwan

Most of the world's mountain-bike factories are Taiwanese. Over half of the world's mountain-bike frames are currently built there, and many of the components too. Taiwan has begun to face stiff competition from China, though, and may lose the number-one spot before long.

HARDTAIL HEAVEN

Most people, in most places, ride hardtail bikes. They have suspension forks on the front, but no travel at the rear. Why are these bikes so popular?

- *They're cheaper* - Hardtails are easier to build and there are less components. You get more bike for your money.
- *You know they work* - The designs have been developed over decades, so with very few exceptions hardtails work well.
- *There's less to go wrong* - The frame of a hardtail is much simpler than a full-suspension bike's, so mechanical problems are less likely to happen.

The biggest difference, though, is that the riding experience on a hardtail is more immediate: you can really feel the ground under you. You have to concentrate harder: hit a rock in the middle of the trail and it'll probably knock you off. This can seem exciting or dangerous, depending on your attitude: it boils down to personal choice.

Groupset: 24 or 27 gears. Some riders just have one ring on the front, and 8 or 9 gears. A few, very fit people even ride fixed-wheel, single-speed bikes.

What's in a Frame?

Frames are made out of loads of different materials, but the three main ones are:

Steel   Back in fashion now because it's a strong material that gives a little under stress.

Aluminum   6061 and 7005 are the most common types. Aluminum bikes sometimes have a stiff, harsh ride but are usually lighter than steel.

Titanium   The most expensive of these three frame materials but very popular with those who can afford it, titanium combines the feel of steel with light weight.

Typical Modern Hardtail

Angled top tube: makes it less painful if you fall off!

Short stem: gives an easier riding position and more control.

Wide riser bars: more control and a more relaxed riding position.

Aluminium frame: 6061 or 7005 are the most common grades.

Aheadset: allows quick changing of forks and easy maintenance.

Pedals: clipless or flat – personal choice.

V-brakes: some bikes use V-brakes, which are light and simple. Many now use disc brakes, which are heavier but far more powerful.

Lightweight wheels: heavier wheels are used for downhill.

Disc breaks: These apply stopping power through pads to the disc, rather than the rim, to stop the bike.

9

FULL SUSPENSION

Today you're more likely to meet a full-suspension bike out on the trail than ever before. They used to be ridden only by downhill freaks. So what changed: why are full-sus bikes so popular now?

- Cross-country full-suspension bikes are now super light: maybe 1 pound (500 g) heavier than an equivalent hardtail.
- Fans of full suspension argue that the increased grip given by the suspension makes them faster, even if they're a little heavier.
- The designs are now well developed: they're efficient and you can buy from well-known companies with confidence that the bike will work.
- They're more comfortable to ride for a whole day.

How to Choose

Here are a few guidelines that could help you choose your first full-suspension bike:

- Pick a bike made by a well-known company, ideally one whose bikes you've ridden before and liked.

- Choose a simple design that you can set up and ride without fiddling with it all the time.

- Make sure you test ride the bike. Any good bike shop will let you do this: some even have off-road areas you can use.

Rear shock: these are either air-sprung or work using a powerful metal spring to absorb shocks.

Wide handlebar for better control.

Front shocks: these are usually balanced against the rear shock, which means they need to offer similar levels of shock absorption and performance. This helps make the bike easy to control.

Rear swing-arm: the lighter, the better! Unless the swing-arm is light, the bike will be hard to drag uphill.

Low standover height: safer in crashes.

Disc brakes

Pivot for rear suspension: This is the most crucial part of the design: if it's in the wrong place, the bike rides very strangely.

Clipless or flat pedals.

RIDING: FREERIDE

All freeriding means is just getting out on your bike and riding over, around, or through whatever you meet. You can ride downhill, uphill, down drop-offs, through single track, on fire roads, on your local trails, or 30 miles (50 km) from home. It's all freeride.

Freeride Checklist

❏ Water bottle or water-carrying backpack

❏ Waterproof shirt

❏ Warm clothes, fleece is best since it doesn't absorb water

❏ Tools, at *least*: puncture kit, spare inner tube, chain splitter, tire levers, Allen keys

❏ Sunscreen if you're going out on a sunny day

❏ Warm gloves and a hat that fits under your helmet if it's cold

What makes freeriding different is the attitude that the riders carry with them in their heads. This can best be summed up in one word: extreme. If you're out freeriding, you're not out for a quiet day in the countryside. You're chasing the biggest adrenaline rush you can find, looking for the fastest, steepest, and most difficult routes.

Jargon Buster

Single track A trail wide enough to fit one bike, and only one bike, at a time. Very exciting to ride: you often can't see far ahead, obstacles jut out into your path, and you're constantly having to react to the route.

What to Ride

There isn't a particular kind of bike for freeriding, though almost all bikes have front suspension. The most important thing is to be sure your bike is strong and safe: if you're riding fast, scary routes, you don't want your bike to break!

RIDING: DOWNHILL

The thrill of charging full-speed through a narrow lane in the trees, or across the steep, open slope of a mountain, is as exhilarating as snowboarding down a steep slope or surfing in big waves. Welcome to downhill mountain biking.

Many downhill bikers live in ski resorts through the summer. There are two reasons for this. The first is that ski slopes without snow on them make perfect mountain-bike trails. The second is the lifts. Downhill bikes have huge amounts of travel and are very, very heavy, to give them added traction. They're so heavy that they're almost impossible to ride uphill: unless you live near a ski lift, you're in for a lot of pushing!

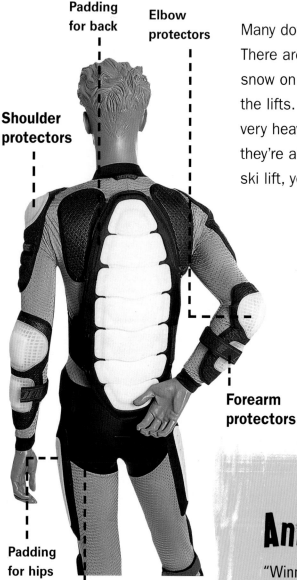

Padding for back

Elbow protectors

Shoulder protectors

Forearm protectors

Padding for hips

Hard plastic plates: protect torso.

Anne-Caroline Chausson

"Winning isn't boring," said the French downhill star Anne-Caroline Chausson in 2002. "When it is, I'll stop." She did a lot of winning. "Anne-Caro" was junior world champion in 1993, 1994, and 1995, then won seven senior world championships between 1997 and 2005. She's the most successful women's downhill racer ever.

WARNiNG!

Downhilling is potentially very dangerous. Riders often walk their route several times before going down it on a bike, and they wear full-body armor and full-face helmets in case they crash. Anyone who thinks they can ride downhill courses without planning the route carefully is likely to end up badly hurt.

15

RIDING: DUAL AND 4X

Dual slalom is like racing your friend around the local woods, except you might win a cup at the end.

Dual slalom and 4x feature two or four riders and are just about the most exciting races to watch. The riders start together and try to make it through the twists and turns as quickly as possible. The course usually features jumps, including doubles, jumps that the most daredevil riders treat as one, leaping the gap between them.

Of course, you don't need a specially prepared course or an organized event for this kind of racing. A local trail that's wide enough for the bikes will do. Get together a group of friends and take it in turns to race each other down the trail. Just make sure too many riders don't go at once and there's enough room for all of you to get down safely.

Brian Lopes – Contest King

Brian Lopes has spent over 10 years at the top of the mountain-bike game. Famous for his amazing acceleration, he won his first World Cup race in 1998, for dual. In 2007, Lopes became the world 4x champion.

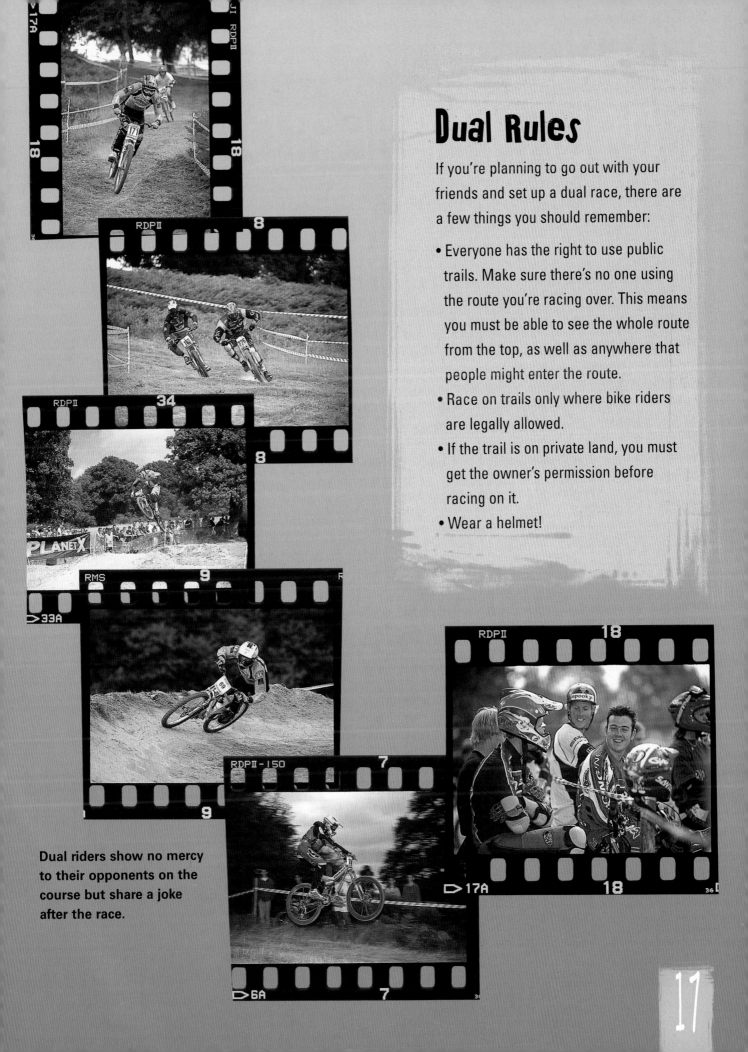

Dual Rules

If you're planning to go out with your friends and set up a dual race, there are a few things you should remember:

• Everyone has the right to use public trails. Make sure there's no one using the route you're racing over. This means you must be able to see the whole route from the top, as well as anywhere that people might enter the route.

• Race on trails only where bike riders are legally allowed.

• If the trail is on private land, you must get the owner's permission before racing on it.

• Wear a helmet!

Dual riders show no mercy to their opponents on the course but share a joke after the race.

RIDING:
URBAN FREERIDE

Would you like to ride sideways along a wall? Up and down a tree trunk? Or maybe hopping between two picnic tables is your thing. This is the crazy world of urban freeriding!

Urban freeriders look at the landscape in the same way skateboarders do: every obstacle becomes an opportunity to perform a trick. Stairs are there to be ridden down; park benches to be jumped; walls to bunny hop; narrow alleys to be wheelied. One thing that's important, though, is showing consideration for other people. However much fun you're having, make sure you're not ruining someone else's day by riding your bike in an inappropriate place.

No-footed endo.

Manual curb hop.

Subway step leap.

19

TECHNIQUE: HILLS

Different riders have very different riding styles: some are super smooth, others seem to wrestle their bikes up and down hills as though they're in a fight. Most people, of course, fall somewhere between the two. Whatever your riding style, whether you're going uphill or down there are a few tips that help even the best riders go faster.

How to do it, shown above, and how not to do it, most definitely shown on the right.

Uphill

DO: Try to stay sitting down on steep slopes: it gives good grip and smooth acceleration.

DON'T: Stand out of the saddle and push hard on the pedals: the back wheel will slide around and you'll tire very quickly.

DO: Keep your weight balanced over the bike: lean into the slope and bend your arms to stop the back wheel lifting up.

DON'T: Pull back hard on the handlebars to try and put power into your pedaling: you'll do a wheelie and land on your back.

Downhill

DO: Wear glasses or something to prevent your eyes from becoming irritated and tearing so that you can see where you're going.

DO: Keep a firm grip on the handlebars.

DON'T: Try to change gear in a bumpy or twisty downhill section: next thing you know you'll be lying in the bushes wondering if anything is broken.

DO: Keep your weight centered on the bike: this means shifting it backward through steeper sections. Both wheels will grip evenly.

DON'T: Put your weight forward: you might go flying over the handlebars if you hit anything.

DO: Control your speed going into tricky areas or places where you can't see what lies ahead.

DON'T: Assume that what's ahead will be as easy as what you're riding on now.

TECHNIQUE: JUMPING

Deliberately trying to leave the ground on a bicycle, which after all is mainly designed to stay on the ground, sounds like a pretty stupid thing to do. But it can make your riding safer: sometimes it's much better to leap over a difficult patch of ground than it is to ride across it. To be able to do this, you have to practice. Try jumping off little curbs and drop-offs that you could easily ride down first, before building up to larger obstacles.

3 Land smoothly, with a big smile.

2 Let the back wheel follow the front off the ground.

1 Lift the front wheel.

Some riders/crazies make jumping their main aim. These riders perform tricks with names like no-footer, no-handed seat grab and, best of all, suicide air. Jumping crazies will risk life and limb to provide a spectacular picture (as you can see from the photo on the right).

WARNING!

Jumping is DANGEROUS. Take great care if you decide you want to try to learn, and get help from someone who knows what they're doing.

COMPETITIONS

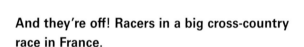

And they're off! Racers in a big cross-country race in France.

As in any sport, mountain bikers have always wanted to try to find out who's the best, and competition has always been part of the mountain-bike scene. There are local, regional, and international races in lots of disciplines. Cross-country, downhill, dual slalom, trials, jumping... if you can put a name to it, there's a competition for it somewhere. Cross-country mountain biking is even part of the Olympics.

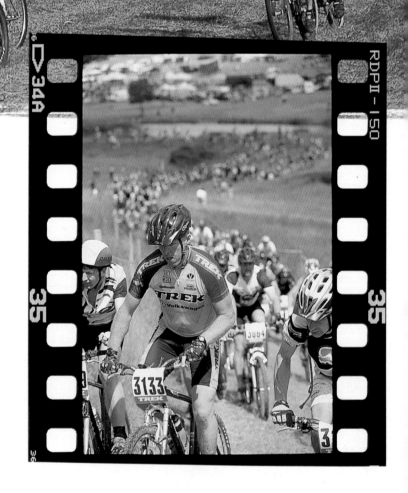

Recently there has been a growth of "alternative" competitions, which are a little different from the traditional ones. Among the most popular of these is the 24-hour marathon race, in which teams of riders race in relays for 24 hours: whichever team has gone farthest in the time is the winner. Also increasing in popularity are adventure-racing triathlons, in which competitors do an open-water swim, a mountain-bike ride, and a cross-country run.

Mud-man racer looks glad to have finished.

World Cup and World Championships

The mountain-biking World Cup is a series of races held through the year. Riders' scores in each race are added together at the end of the season to decide who is the World Cup winner. But the end of the season also sees the World Championships: a one-off race in which the winner becomes world champion.

A running start to a 24-hour relay race.

25

In mountain biking, the biggest stars of all are the downhill racers. And once in a while, a downhill racer comes along who's so good, even the other riders don't think he or she can be beaten. These are the world's fastest riders, the downhill legends.

Nicolas Vouilloz: Nico, as he is known, had one of the world's best runs from 1992 until 2002. He won junior and senior world championships a record 10 times, and took several World Cup overall championships as well. In 2003, he tried a career in the World Rally Championships and raced as a semiprofessional.

Anne-Caroline Chausson: A top rider at the same time as Nicolas Vouilloz, find out more about Anne-Caro on page 14.

Sabrina Jonnier: After Anne-Caroline's last world title in 2005, the competition to grab her crown in 2006 was hotter than a smoking frying pan full of oil. Sabrina won and continued winning the next year, too. She looks set to carry on at the top of the sport for many years to come.

Still Want to Become a Professional?

Nicolas Vouilloz was the most successful rider ever in downhill, which is the most popular and visually exciting form of mountain biking. But in 1999, he lost his sponsor, Sunn, and had to enter races without a team backing him up and without being paid. However good you are, being a professional mountain biker is not an easy way to earn a living.

Sam Hill: The same year that Sabrina Jonnier won her first senior world title, Sam Hill came to the fore in the men's event. And like Sabrina, he won again in 2007. Sam faced stiff competition from riders such as Fabien Barel of France, who won the world title in 2003 and 2004, but at times during the 2007 season, he reached a near Vouilloz state of better-than-everyone-ness.

> **"** It definitely happened a lot quicker than I imagined. It's always been my dream to make a living from racing my bike, so it's something I've worked hard for. There is always someone... that I want to beat, so I think I try to step it up at every race. **"**

– Sam Hill explains what it's like to become the world's best downhill racer.

ETHICS AND SAFETY

All this high-octane fun is great, but unless you're on a race course, you're probably sharing your riding area with other outdoor enthusiasts. There are certain things you need to do to make sure you don't ruin their fun: it can be quite shocking to have a mountain bike whizz past at 30 miles per hour (50 km/h) when you're out for a quiet day in the country.

Mountain bikers already have a bad reputation, especially with walkers. Only by being extra polite can we start to change this. If you think it doesn't matter, you're wrong: if mountain bikers continue to be seen as dangerous and selfish trail users, they will end up being banned from more and more places. In the end, there won't be anywhere good to ride.

It's a WHAT?

Good Image Advice

• Only ride where you're allowed to.

• Always slow down or stop for walkers and horses to avoid scaring them: it's easy to get back up to speed afterward.

• Greet people you meet with a smile, and thank anyone who stops for you or opens a gate.

• It's a good idea to have a bell on your bike to warn people saying you're about to overtake them. If you don't have a bell, be polite. Saying "Excuse me" or "Watch out" will do.

Safety Checklist

See the box in the Freeride section, on page 12–13, for a list of things you should take out biking with you.

Signs for posted mountain-bike routes ("VTT" stands for "bikes for all terrain" in French) in the Alps.

Enviro Biking

Bicycles are good for the environment, right? Well, yes and no. They don't use fossil fuels that cause pollution, but they can have a negative effect. Everyone who uses the outdoors – bikers, walkers, runners, horses – wears away a little soil as they pass. Mountain bikes aren't the worst offenders at this, but there are a couple of things you can do to cut down the amount of soil erosion you cause:

1. Stick to marked trails, so that erosion can be controlled by those who manage the trail.

2. Try not to skid your bike: the sliding tire rips grass and soil loose.

How not to do it: that dust is soil, which will be blown away in the wind.

GLOSSARY

adrenaline (uh-DREH-nuh-lun) A hormone produced by your body in exciting circumstances.

BMX (bee-em-EX) Short for "bicycle motocross."

bunny hop (BU-nee HOP) A small jump used by mountain bikers to clear obstacles.

clipless pedals (KLIP-les PEH-dulz) Pedals that attach to the sole of your shoe using a clamp.

motocross (MOH-toh-kros) Motorcycle racing around a specially prepared off-road course.

shock (SHOK) A suspension unit that allows the wheels to move up and down under pressure.

ski lift (SKEE LIFT) A lift that transports skiers up the slopes of a mountain. The most common kinds are chairs strung from a cable and enclosed cabins.

sponsor (SPON-ser) Someone or something who pays an athlete to enter competitions and do photo shoots in return for publicity.

wheelie (HWEE-lee) Riding along with the front wheel of your bike in the air.

FURTHER INFORMATION

Books to Read

Gifford, Clive. *Mountain Biking.* North Mankato, MN: Smart Apple Media, 2006.

MacAulay, Kelley and Bobbie Kalman. *Extreme Mountain Biking.* New York: Crabtree Publishing, 2006.

Mason, Paul. *Diary of a BMX Freak.* Mankato, MN: Capstone, 2005.

Web Sites

Due to the changing nature of Internet links, PowerKids Press has developed an online list of Web sites related to the subject of this book. This site is updated regularly. Please use this link to access the list:
www.powerkidslinks.com/limit/biking/

INDEX